WHY? Wandering Thoughts

Holly Harding

Published by New Generation Publishing in 2020

Copyright © Holly Harding 2020

First Edition

The author asserts the moral right under the Copyright, Designs and Patents Act 1988 to be identified as the author of this work.

All Rights reserved. No part of this publication may be reproduced, stored in a retrieval system or transmitted, in any form or by any means without the prior consent of the author, nor be otherwise circulated in any form of binding or cover other than that in which it is published and without a similar condition being imposed on the subsequent purchaser.

ISBN: 978-1-80031-675-1

www.newgeneration-publishing.com

New Generation Publishing

Prologue / Bio

These floating thoughts have been written down in challenging circumstances. I barely survived a severe car crash (1970), caused by a drunk driver on a German motorway, in coma, with multiple brain damage, of which two are of relevance here. First, my memory was gone. The content of my then just acquired master's degree in Philosophy and Literature of Germanic Languages was left behind on the German grass on which I was thrown out of the car, after breaking the windshield with my head, plunged into the deep besides the motorway. I still have no recollection of my studies. Secondly, my cerebral eyesight was damaged so I could no longer read, it would get me 'seasick' and aggravate my ever present headache, still going on. These thoughts I gathered 25 years later on, with almost closed eyes, one paragraph each day. A few years ago, I found out that I started to be able to read but only on an iPad, no printed texts, no laptops... So now, 50 years after the accident, I proudly want to publish the text.

Nevertheless, I had managed to raise our two daughters to high standards. They were excellent students and are now very successful lawyers. Besides Belgium, we lived in Surrey, UK, and New Jersey, USA. The girls went to school and University in all three countries.

We have three wonderful grandchildren: two Americans and one Flemish toddler.

Over the years after the accident, I developed an interest in painting. Starting from scratch (literally!), my work became more refined. The painting on the cover (by me, helena m.) illustrates my wandering of thoughts.

I have the swift ability to step in and out of my dreamworld.

As some philosophers proclaimed the indisputable existence of two levels of worlds long before me, I agree on the number, not on their intrinsic value. Their worlds consisted of either bare phenomena versus abstract order or faint appearances versus their ideal originals. Mine are simply every day's painful reality versus the honey-filled sweetness of chosen characters and events. The latter always happened to be linked together in a rather fortunate way.

The weather is at a standstill, deciding on the next attack. After an unseasonable period of frostbite followed by torrential rains spilling into floods there are only a few more vicious options left. Even nature is holding its breath anxiously trying not to drop a pine-pin in order not to inspire any weather system. It is like watching a cheap movie-set where they have forgotten to plug in the ventilator for gradual storm-building.

On top of that it is the 1st of January. The evening news is advertising all your typical first-day-of-the-year-events as there seems to have been held a ski-jumping and a marathon somewhere in this celebrating world. My brand-new-year day consisted of family visits which turned out to be far less irritating than similar ones in the past. In fact I remember some of those house calls to bluntly be horrifying with great-aunts and uncles, stricken in years, squeezing smiles on their faces and presenting a chair with their bony, crooked fingers. The wishing-well visit used to last for two hours in which period the children were allowed two cookies. They probably meant well. It is hard to imagine them young and playful.

The next day the weather woke up long before me. Experiencing another splash outside, I decide on making it a comfortable day in. There is even this ever growing urge to reproduce on canvas what had been created in my mind a while ago. That's how I operate as a painter: I have these powerful outbursts of creativity, which result in a parade of fully finished paintings in my mind. The agony starts when I ultimately proceed to the painstaking task of accurately duplicating my mind's creation on the canvas. Preparing for a painting session, I gladly accept my daughter's offer to take over dinner cooking at the appropriate time. After a few hours of intense struggling, I finally deliver the foundation of what is to become the significant background of the new painting. Exhausted and only partially happy with the result, which has to be said is a common reaction for me, I indulge in the stilling sound of metrical Latin-American music. I am fully aware of the fact that the appeasing condition is only effective during a few rounds of this music. After an extended exposure to these sounds the already stretched nerves can eventually get prickled into a lamentable condition.

In the meantime the new year is establishing itself rather smoothly. As was to be expected, the invitations are rolling in at a steady pace. The whole month of January is being booked by anxious family. The Latin-American music is on again and it is being obvious that the relaxing effect will last for much longer if not preceded by a painting session.

Since the writing started, I find myself as locked in an ambiguous situation. When writing I feel some sort of guilt for not being painting and vice versa. A lot can be said in favour of writing versus painting: you get to organizing your thoughts and feelings, rearranging your priorities and slowly digesting what has been eating at you simply by putting it in words. Once the text is staring at you, the expressed problem suddenly appears already dealt with and sometimes even not worthwhile the sheer thought of it. This of course proves the therapeutic effect of writing and therefore part of its popularity. Painting on the other hand offers you the overwhelming power of almost instantly creating beauty for both eye and mind. The strength of a baroque or a pale palette drives your mind as with gentle lashes, a caressing whip. Shapes and symbols, figures and lines picture themselves into a born concept or emotion.

The peculiar thing is that although I show signs of eagerly ambitious competition between writing and painting, my true fulfillment has always been sealed in sifting and raveling music. The result would be a scale of emotions and ideas which in their turn could trigger inspiration towards painting and writing. At this very moment Rachmaninov's second piano concerto is playing. In the third movement the theme is being presented alternately by violins and piano: are these instruments supplementing each other like marriage partners or are they defying each other like duelists? As a former violin and piano player I find it extremely difficult to award a preference to one of both instruments. If completely honest I, maybe reluctantly, have to admit the grandeur of the piano standing tall on its own against the group of violins. Sensations arisen during former performances of Rachmaninov's fascinating music have been captured on canvas in my early painting days. Because of the totally captivating aspect of music which allows you to completely drown in it, I consider music the most sublime of all arts.

What makes the position of art in life so valuable, is the fact that art has been established by a driving force from within the artist rather than coming from someone ordering or imposing it. The impact on the art-lover therefore whirls down in a pure and unconditional way: the mere merit of the artist being translated in sheer delight for the art-lover.

I can get inspired by beauty, any beauty, in things, never in persons. I have not been too fortunate with the people surrounding me especially during teenage-years. A lot of psychological debris still remains to be cleared away, every so often popping up in nightmares. Anyway, having growing up daughters gives me the unique opportunity of vividly and happily living through teenage-years again not only as a mother but almost as a sister as well.

Today after another painting session I feel exhausted, completely drained as is usual for me in those circumstances. I feel like being empty, hollow, like a cartoon character consisting of a coincidence of lines, like a walking question mark. This rather poor health-condition is the result of a car-accident caused by a drunken driver some twenty-four years ago. I came out of a coma to go on with a totally different life. Ever since the accident I never lived one single day without headaches, often pounding and I experienced a steadily worsening nagging neck pain. I had to learn to live with facial scars too. The sympathy and needed support you would expect from friends and family were virtually non-existing. Only my mother who overcame the accident with painful but curable injuries is aware of my ordeal and offers help where ever she can. My husband and daughters, whom I met and had many years later, are very supportive too. The four of us are so close and loving, spreading happiness to each other.

The painting does not really come out as I would have liked. Not that it is incorrigible, but still far from the previewed end result. It is a stressing work process trying to capture and reproduce in a minute fashion what had been fully established in the creative mind. Don't means often fail? Isn't the abstract mind always being superior to the executing forces? But then again what is the abstract mind worth without its translation into perceptible terms? Is this the focus point of the intellectual's agony, the daily struggle to have the mind's activity fit into a world that is operating on routine and intrinsic basic language?

Tomorrow is my birthday. Last year I wrote down these observations:

It's my birthday again. As a little girl I used to cherish my birthday. As a sacred space in time I would worship the mere existence of that day. The celebration was of my own making. Every year I would climb my throne and preside my whole small world that was completely unaware though of this supremacy. The importance of my birthday must have found its base in the fact that I myself didn't really own much, never have, never will. The toys that we shared really belonged to my sister, well for seventy-five per cent that is. The other twenty-five per cent were either already used up or broken anyway. My very own possessions, which I kept as relics, except for my dolls and some bigger toys, perfectly fitted into two medium size biscuit-tins and even left ample space for potential future gifts. So my birthday was really mine, no one could deprive me of it.

I have to keep on writing since the computer is beginning to develop a will of its own as it were. First refusing to stock additional notes, it now begins to wonder which text at all it is supposed to go on remembering. While typing these words, I telepathically try to remind the rules of the game to this technical genius, recalling its sort of sworn duty to mankind. It works; we are friends again.

Something I do experience, very explicitly, is the fact that when writing you are as if retreating in your own world, where there isn't even room for children or a husband. They seem like a hundred miles away and hardly known. At the computer or handling a brush I am a completely different person. It is like, apparently out of the blue, having to go on in a glass-bell or air-bubble. Everything seems slightly unreal and rather hushed or dimmed. Senses don't get stimulated and the mind's work obtains absolute priority. You realize your individuality as well as your independence as a human creature. Is it from within that we get to socialize with others and become involved or is it utter pressure from society itself to mingle? Is this the reason why artists are pretty reluctant to throw themselves as it were into the outer world?

I would describe the establishing of a relationship with marriage as a prospective in a similar fashion. Like the mating season for animals, youth is the time in human life where efforts are made to finally focus on the right partner. The young person would cover him/herself as it were with an outer shield which is strewed with transmitters and receivers. Signals come and go. The two who share most signals are most likely to end up together. After marriage though and its expansion towards a family, the shield loses its purpose. The two persons formerly drawn to each other start to run down the transmitters and receivers and eventually the shield. They regress in a way within themselves, leaving two separate nuclei, two cores that still can communicate but not necessarily do or have to.

I have spent a one hour sleep night due to fierce pain attacks so I decided to spoil myself with a few extra hours of rest after everybody had left the house for work or school. When I woke up the day had settled quite nicely. It looks icy cold but the sun is still climbing and working on it. What I now see is leaving me in awe. Out of one of the three bedroom windows overlooking the garden, my eagerly wandering eye falls upon one of the hundred trees living in the garden and the adjacent wood. The spotted tree, a perfect pine, is covered with melting ice that is busy gathering at the end of a twig. The ever expanding drop, dangling diffidently and full of fear of heights, catches the sunlight and starts to show itself off in any colour of the spectrum. On other branches and twigs the same procedure follows, leaving the whole tree looking like a natural phenomenal Christmas tree. Next to the tree the sunbeams stretch towards the ground in purpose of safely escorting the possibly descending fairy who would come and collect the colourful balls. Or are the beams inviting me to adventurously climb up towards the inspiring sun? If I would feel more reposed right now, I surely would consider to give it a try!

A few days later. Since there is no imminent danger of severe winter weather I psychologically am preparing for spring. Nature agrees and even starts to show some very shy blossoms, probably only to regret after a short while. But then again nature never learns, making the same mistake over and over again, as do its creatures great or small, supposedly wise or not.

Why is it that good intentions are doomed virtually always to be taken the wrong way even by people who should know you better? Do the others all have devious characters or is it sheer madness in this day and age to have them let alone show them? I am a crusader, in the naive sense of the word, sailing to have truth and honesty prevail, to help find happiness. Unfortunately, I never earned any respect in doing so, I even get ridiculed or condemned by my own people. Sheer madness but by whom?

Tonight and tomorrow are reserved to family, tonight the in-laws, tomorrow my own family. They all make a bunch of stereotypes with one thing in common: they take themselves so seriously, they consider themselves as of immense value to the family, community, society, the world for that matter. Here again my mother is the exception. Even if tempted, I would never actually throw them on canvas, they might come out in a fairly unattractive way.

The orchid branch on my desk is looking grim, casting away its flowers, obviously in distress by what is written down.

The weekend is over, it turned out all right. Reason for this open social approach of mine was the satisfying notion that the ever so demanding labour of producing a painting had finally been successful. Well it means that the painting is finished but not necessarily to my liking. The painting is to be called Flowers on Trash; the trash turned out fine, the flowers less so.

It just so happens that the next weekend too has been almost fully booked by the in-laws. They seem to like the company. I start feeling tempted to have all of them read this text in order to restore quiet weekends. Most of them are probably basically all right, very basically that is.

Where on earth do I have to reside to find at least some kindred spirits? Or are these only to be found as spectres in the dark velvet of the night, reflecting like mirrors your very own emotions, thoughts and

questions? What is real and what is
only thought to be? Even facts in
their sheer happening are vulnerable
to various interpretations and
reactions. And yet religions are
claiming that every step of the way
had been decided beforehand. This
includes every one and only choice
made by any individual in the
colossal amount of options
concerning conclusions and
decisions triggered by or simply
succeeding events. Isn't the next
question obvious? Is one truth
existing or happening or are there as
many truths as living or witnessing
people? Is it not an awful lot of
people's business in their life and
work to create some order in the
chaos of truths and nothing but the
truths? What a waste of time or is
it? What else would people be doing
rather than reorganizing what seemed
to have derailed? Maybe they could
work more towards the future, be
more inventive in ameliorating every
day life? But then again why bother,
we merely are a type of evolved and
therefore complicated plant, living
by seasons, coming, flourishing and
going.

Yet another question that has been
popping up in my mind every so often
is about the meaning and function
of colours in life and the world.
Are they descriptive or are they

categorical? Are they invented and used by the mind in an artistic fashion? Or are they some sort of chemical illustrations from a cosmic point of view of the categories existing in life and others created in society? If they are invented, can we be certain that we all observe them in the same way? Probably not because even interminable definitions in general, let alone the ones describing colours, use words which in their turn sin against the same doubtful rules of exactness and clarity. If from out of the universe they depict categories in life and society, it would be possible that the shy were pink and the exuberant were red, dancers were green, lawyers blue, dentists white, mothers yellow, priests purple etc… The trick would be to accumulate as many allocated colours as possible in order to spark off an ever growing value in life and society. Reaching the full spectrum then would be the ultimate achievement. The same theory could be applicable to sounds and shapes. Maybe a doctor is an a-flat in cosmic terms and a photographer would be a cone whereas the conductor in fact is a triangle. Adding all this up can lead us towards a somehow organized cosmic chaos: a continuous whirl of all these combined symbols existing next to each other, portraying a universal scale picture only as such perceptible by a genius. What a waste of energy if the genius got already bored with the view ages ago and took the rest of the universal time off. We would then call the earth a merry-go-round spinning off into space with no apparent purpose at all.

Life back in Belgium is beginning to weigh very heavily on me. Seven months have gone by since we left the United States where I, my husband and two daughters have lived for two years. The enthusiasm of the girls over there was so inspiring, whereas their visible unhappiness over here is depressing. They dream of going back to the States and there is almost nobody here to be found who could bring himself to agree on their preference. Over here life in the States is considered to be of a lesser quality: there is supposedly lack of culture and tradition, which of course the whole of Western Europe is so proud to offer in abundance. Europeans plainly brag of their ancestors' accomplishments who are often the same people most Americans descend from. The last century for that matter did not produce a lot in Europe to boast. Furthermore there would be the drug and drug related problems in the States; criminality is high, moral standards and education are poor. True in many cases but at least the Americans acknowledge the problems and are fervently looking for solutions. Europe's principles and moral values too are declining rapidly but officials and responsible people stay on their high horses denying any trouble far below. Despicable conduct and profligacy are on the increase in Europe, which, if not taken care of, could undermine Europe's legacy of judgment and wisdom.

Who on the other hand could deny the American people's sense of pioneering and ambitious enterprising, their vitality and their zeal?

Why is it that bliss strikes on a tiny scale only? Is it because of the earth's insignificant position in universe that only scanty gratifying events are being shed upon its habitants. If you string all every day's fortunate moments though, you may still end up with a fair share of potential happiness. It is everybody's challenge then to pick and mould the right experiences into a suitably satisfying state of mind. Happiness is never offered as such, it originates and, if well kept, is able to grow or expand.

Evil is just the flip side of goodness like ugliness is the down side of beauty. Sometimes it is only the spur of the moment mood which makes us decide on acting or evaluating either way. The mere changing of mood can toss the imaginative coin and show the other side. It is like the expression on the face of a clown, smiling or crying according to the stage of the story: very explicit but yet so volatile.

I treated myself to a bunch of mini tulips today. Most of the carmine flowers landed on my desk in an old cut glass vase. The sunshine gets caught in between the ribs and cuddles the stems. One of the flowers rather bluntly decides to leave the formation and bends forward in order to gather any information on what I am doing on the PC.

Today I learned more about those staggering cosmic proportions like the sun being eight speed of light minutes away whereas some stars are at a distance of several billion light-years. It is facts like these that make human life look so ridiculous and absurd. Only one aspect on this earth is standing irrefutably tall in comparison to this immensity and that is mother's love. This love is so all-embracing and unconditional no matter how severe the attacks towards the children, no matter how vicious the attackers. So precious with no equal it is being passed on from mother to daughter to remain on this earth for as long as the earth itself continues to be. You would even be inclined to think that a grain of cosmic infinity, dropped on earth at its origin, is responsible for this almost superhuman size quality. Or was it a snip or shred of universal planning that whirled down on earth forever programming this vast love in motherhood.

I went through a momentous experience these past few days.

As my uncle died, I was confronted with those considerations that try to deal with the meaning of life itself. What on earth are we doing on earth? Why are we here if it is only for such an insignificant period of time during which we are submitted to the most circumstantial circumstances? Laughing, talking, deciding and being dead the next moment can not be the result of ultimate cosmic planning! Or is it a minute piece of the universal jigsaw that would be missed if not present? Anyhow it is one familiar face less in the course of life. Another personality moves status from active functioning towards being stored into passive memory of the temporary survivors. Those who loved him will cherish him in vivid remembrance, others will have him quickly degrade to database.

I had a funny thought today: when thinking too much, your brain could easily get overworked and lose weight!

In the meanwhile I got two paintings ready to be sent to the Royal Academy's Summer Exhibition. I love them both although I have a slight preference for CHESS AND CHERRY over FLOWERS ON TRASH. It would be nice of course if I would not be the only one to appreciate them.

What a day again! Spring in the air, battlefield on the ground! Life is an illness, the moment you are born you get contaminated. The disease develops steadily during the course of years. It is a struggle for survival against the meanest attacks. They come from everywhere and they are always called: people! Life is like a bullfight; no matter how brave and proud, the bull has to go down in the end. The sad thing is that, by standing tall against his fierce and savage attackers, without knowing, the bull itself determines the duration of the slaughter. Humans at least have an option to bail out; they can decide on ending their lives gracefully before any more harm can be inflicted. So you get rid of those nasty people but you say eternally goodbye too to everything else basically being the goodies of nature. Except for people there are a lot of heartwarming events coming your way every day and if you are able to assess them properly they virtually all can bring power of freedom and happiness into your life. Like the shy pale female pheasant who in a panic-stricken hurry crossed the lawn in a flash, leaving me watching from the window, in an uneasy mood of surrounding threat, only to stop suddenly and start pecking in the most relaxed way. Or the ducks, the other day, who just got married and on their search for privacy miscalculated from the air, obviously due to myopia and landed coarsely on a three square feet rain pool on the lawn, missing the somewhat larger pond close by.

Cynical as they may sound, today I need to make these observations: if you, my unknown friend, have the privilege to be born immersed by honesty both in searching and doing, you are doomed to be damned. Nobody can live up to you, they are all so detestably small. If on top of that they are too egoistic to care, you will find yourself being slaughtered over and over and over again throughout your life in their own despicable self defense. The linked loneliness is the only thing worse than physical pain, however bad itself. Therefore, my dear unknown friend, from the bottom of my heart, I wish you a very short life!

A few days later, a more positive note demands its full rights too. At this exact time in the course of my life, I lived through, not the perfect, but the most possibly human of days. This was the day that takes a bit of everything: emotions, fears, hopes, intellectual challenge, psychological insight, an unexpectedly friendly conversation with strangers, comforting words, a compliment about your appearance, appreciation for a job well done: a nice life in a nutshell. If every day could be as loaded, we could live a damn whole lot of lives. We could collect and cherish them. Everybody could feel rich and significant.

Today it is snowing, one week after Easter. You would think weather systems existing for millions of years, they would know by now what the seasons actually mean and should provide. With shoots and sprigs budding, nature is extremely vulnerable and yet nature sends these killing snowdrops on these young lives. They come down in countless quantities, swelling and growing confident on their downward journey, aiming grimly and freezing their victims on the ground. That is where their pride ends. After their deadly mission they completely disappear as if they had never existed, but leaving a trace of destruction behind. I can't help but drawing a parallel with human race, some beings out to destroy others.

Normally there are all sorts of creatures running and jumping through the garden: rabbits, squirrels, pheasants, deer, all kinds of birds but right now only blackbirds are on the scene, hunting earthworms. So what is a bad day for almost everyone, including the worms, turns out to be a day of feast and banquet for the blackbirds. It is always a mixed bag: some win, some lose. Only when winners remain winners and losers remain losers it gets boring especially for the latter.

After a late flu-attack, I find myself spaced-out by both the antibiotics and my daily headaches flaring up violently. The end of April is hardly the time for the flu but considering the weather it was no surprise. When your body is in pain it is amazing how it seems to grow. Suddenly it takes on huge proportions like your aching head reaches the size of an excavating machine, functioning in an equally subtle way too. A stress struck stomach feels more like a hot-air balloon and even an infectious little finger expands towards ancient Greek statue measures. Fever equals a furnace and your heartbeat competes with Beethoven's worst passages. Amazing how the body can completely take over, leaving the suppressed mind in no position at all. Able to reproduce only mental convulsions, the poor spirit must wait until the body is willing to delegate supremacy again. When that time comes, the mind usually prevails in a purified condition, like it had been treated and cured itself. Since tomorrow will be the last day of the antibiotics therapy (for the time being), I am curious to find out how purified my spirit has become in the process!

Today is a glorious day, plenty of sunshine without any cloud. When you live in Belgium you quickly learn that the only certainty of a sunny day is when there is absolutely no single cloud in the sky. Because if there is even just one tiny little nasty thing to be spotted, it is guaranteed to hurry and install itself right in front of the mighty sun and it will stay there for the rest of the day. Of course this has no scientific ground, weather systems don't work that way but Belgium does. Anything that can go wrong or sour does so in Belgium. Wouldn't it be nice if we just could erase it from every world map and simply forget about it. If scattered over the entire world, Belgians won't cause much hurt. They are basically harmless people and they mean well and not even that. On top of that Belgians don't really exist since there are only Flemings (57 % of the population), Walloons, the ones living in Brussels (who could belong to any race) and the German speaking community who were made to join Belgium after World War 1.

Another glorious day! All of a sudden the lawn seems a lot smaller since the shrubs and bushes bulge with joy and health, embracing the first significant sunshine this year.

With the prospect of fine weather it is understandable that we like to hurry towards the summer as a safeguard. But the reflex of rushing is effective the whole year round, even towards winter. Why are we in a hurry to get through the years and reach the end of our lives. Isn't it because of a flaw in our ability, or lack of, to control time? We can't but move in one direction and speed, we have no other option or choice. Where the place-experience is concerned, we can walk free any way we want, we can even go back. Therefore there is a discrepancy between the time and place dimensions, which in my view is due only to a still inadequate approach of our mind to the concept time itself. The aptitude to fully comprehend the notion "time" probably lies in the still undeveloped part of our brain. This relatively enormous brain-space yet to be put into use is indeed potentially offering a capability of fundamentally pushing back many scientific limits. We were born much too soon!

Why is it that real dumb people always are looking for a culprit for everything that goes wrong. They use two basic rules to identify the guilty person: it is never themselves or one of their buddies and secondly, it is always somebody they are extremely jealous of. In their stupid mind this is a way of leveling with their " superior ". How to explain that civilisation in its own right is running in the right direction whereas " the so called civilised people " are running in the opposite one these days. Instead of learning they forget, instead of progressing they choose the passive pace of trampling on the spot or even regressing. They prefer cheap pleasure to value and they replace principles by trendy gang rules. Anything to belong and be popular. From that point of view we were born too late, so on the whole this must be the right time to live, believe it or not!

Two weeks from now I will learn from the Royal Academy in London whether one of my paintings has been accepted for showing in the Summer Exhibition. No need to describe the honour and pride accompanying an admission. A wonderful feeling of accomplishment and fulfillment would probably immediately trigger the next inspiration towards a new creation.

Talking about inspiration, there is this divinely scenting bunch of lilies of the valley flaunting defiantly on my desk, almost forcing me into something creative. They come out of my parents' garden where they had a wonderful time growing with sunshine, shade and wind protection as needed and welcome.

The ducks are back tonight, still as shortsighted as before, missing once again the pond while diving into a rain pool instead. They seem extraordinarily hungry since they almost come knocking on the window asking for food. They have a few slices of bread thrown at them and a few pictures taken while devouring it. Not even the flashes can disturb their meal. Afterwards they take off again into the tempting night.

I have reached the time in my life where I am appreciating the real values, the basics rather than the fringes and the ornaments. Forcing the mind to acknowledge and express its own thoughts brings about a feeling of taking responsibility, not more, not less. This goes further as to every choice we make. Basics are providing solid grounds and offering lasting prospects: they are what you need and if well-chosen they will serve you eternally.

There is a baby rabbit of the dominating kind that is eating away the whole garden. Ambition is healthy but this yuppie rabbit is slightly overdoing it. Chasing away even the largest of birds like magpies and crows it semi officially declared the garden its own territory. It still has the wrong notion of danger but it is bound to learn either the right or the hard way.

Today is Mother's day, that is the strictly commercial one and at the same time the non-religious one. The real traditional and catholic feast of all mothers is still on August 15. My younger daughter is baking what already starts to smell as a delicious apple cake. Tonight the whole family will be going out for dinner, which had been decided long before this day was declared Mother's day or more exactly, before we knew about it. It being Belgian weather again, the choice of the restaurant will be made in function of the proximity of the nearest parking place. Anyway now is cake time when judging the fine aroma filling the house!

Rachmaninov's third piano concerto is playing. If you consider the music well, it occurs that each movement is so full of themes that he easily could have worked them out in thirty more piano concertos; instead he preferred only a few but then bursting with inspiration.

When living in New Jersey, no longer than a year ago, I had the marvelous opportunity of visiting Thomas A. Edison's mansion and factory in Orange several times. Although the pure genius of the inventor was striking enough in every outstanding evidence, the exceptional object that impressed me mostly in the house was the grand piano. It appeared that Rachmaninov himself had been one of the regular houseguests and that he abundantly made use of the piano giving away concerts to the Edison family. What an ultimate joy this must have been to everybody!

Rachmaninov is concluding now in a dramatic swing of octaves, so what better way for me to end this semi-official Mother's day.

I watched a program on television, well part of it, about three generations Somalia men; Grandfather still living in the desert as a nomad, relying on camels for food, transportation and wealth; Father, who went to study in the United States and who is a teacher now in The Netherlands and Son who is 21, chewing, on the dole in Holland and back in Somalia with the sole purpose to visit the family with his father. The confrontation between grandfather and grandson is painful. No common ground, almost no common language and worst of all no common respect. The visit over, the father leaves with dual, ambiguous insight into life. What is the right approach, the purely natural or the cultural one? Where did his intellectual progress leave his son? He even asks the question why people are the only living creatures that spend their lives trying to find out how to live it instead of simply living it!

Some Cretan music is playing. Well actually it is the title soundtrack of a British series located on Crete. As is typical for ancient Greek drama the program bears an ominous narrative supported by both inhospitable surroundings and very basic, original music. The people involved belong to the two categories: the genuine defenders of high morals and principles and on the other hand the fanatically defying ones. Some remnant of old mythology wanders over the story and its participants, judging them by ancient criteria and appropriately awarding or punishing them. The music sounds so menacing it is like throwing a spell over you from which you even don't want to escape. The undergoing of the sounds, the mere submitting to them safeguards in a way. It provides like a protective shell which won't let any harm happen to anyone inside. The result is though that towards the end there are more grieved than rejoicing people. But isn't that the essence of life? Always and everywhere people are causing grief to other people, trying constantly to ruin lives. Why is it that people are out to get each other? Even within family they take a devious pleasure in hurting and insulting. Only nature can bring relief. Although we still don't quite understand every exact functioning of it, we do know nature seldom means badly, if you interpret or receive it properly.

Appreciating music is such a personal affair to which everybody reacts differently. You can't explain music. You can give some sort of guidelines by which a person could become more able to catch structure and harmony. Somebody can be made more receptive towards the essence and coherence of the sounds that ultimately create the melody or theme. But the real effect of music on every individual remains personal, subjective and unique. I can be thrown into ecstasy when hearing a simple, basic tune like the Greek theme and remain untouched by dramatic full orchestra, full chorus performance, or the other way round. It is all in the striking impact of the tones on your emotional, sensual and psychological state of the moment. When this experience is being lifted by intellectual awareness and incorporation the ultimate appreciation is achievable. If on the other hand you would block or close off your susceptible attitude, no charm deriving from music would ever come close to reaching you.

When appreciating a painting the joy is more notion oriented, lies in the personal discovery of the match between its concept and its composition. Then the insight in the artist's creative mind through his painting enlightens and enriches the observer's own mind. The shapes and colours as parts of the painting deliver a challenge as to satisfy the eye and the mind again.

On that aspect it might be daring but feasible to compare William Turner and Sergei Rachmaninov. Turner's concept or vision is standing in perfect harmony with its composition. But the forms and tinges are mostly unexpected but if you consider them well, they are the best choice to support the whole design. Rachmaninov works equivalently: thematic ideas and harmonic structure go hand in hand. On top of that he elegantly alternates majors and minors and elaborates chords in their compound and rhythm to emphasize the elementary theme basis.

Pieter P. Rubens (who by the way lived in Antwerp like I do) and Johann S. Bach on the other hand were totally predictable once their artistic theme was established. No surprises in structure, composition and even final touch. Everything was developed obeying strict classical rules, which were thought to be completely binding. The Impressionists widely opened the gates to let personal engagement and commitment stream through, thereby highlighting the individual perception and thinking.

Tomorrow is the beginning of the week in which the Royal Academy Committee will officially communicate to every contributor its decision on the selection of works for the Summer Exhibition. Of course I am eager to learn whether one of my two paintings has been selected. Anyway I have some marvellous inspiration to work on the coming months. I can no longer imagine my life without this creative drive: it would be dull and incomplete.

A few weeks later; I receive the news that my paintings have been rejected. Although rather disappointing, there was no real surprise in it, especially when a reputed American paper revealed the procedure. At least two-thirds of the chosen paintings for the Exhibition are already allocated opportunities to Academy members, veterans and other privileged people like established foreign and British artists. The "hopeful yet nonestablished artist", who puts his soul on the spot when his not-for-sale creation is presented goes by unnoticed while the jury blinks.

It is a vicious circle: you have to be known to be picked to become known.

Since I constantly notice remarkable differences in daily human behaviour, I try to reach a satisfying explanation. The most plausible is the one that divides people into believers in life after death and the sceptics. The believers think they either have to earn their eternal life and therefore do their best to live to the book (or is it The Book) or are entitled to a compensation for the rotten life they have to endure on earth. The sceptics on the other hand come in three categories. First there are those who make the best of everything in life while it lasts and are even prepared to trespass moral, social and humanitarian boundaries. Secondly there are those who could not care less, who live through the day however it presents itself. They simply carry on till the end. And finally there are the critical intellectuals: since they realize life is all you get, they try to raise the standards, seeking satisfaction in purely exercising principles and values for their own intrinsic merit. If only the world could provide more of these people, it would automatically become a much better place.

All of this leads on to yet another crucial question. Why is there the succession of days and nights? Is it to provoke progress and improvement over and over again, to constantly offer a new chance for doing better? Or are we simply subdued to some sort of cosmic "mechanical" routine that does not even wonder whether a living soul wonders?

When you accept death as an inherent and crucial fact of life especially when you have good reason to think that yours is near, you start to look upon life in a totally different way. All your life you worked on the educated essentials, basics, values, standards and principles as they are established in society. Now comes the time for "details", as they have importance in the whole context of your own personality. For me it means more and more disregarding people and enjoying the silent pleasures of the earth as are to be found in nature. They are so pure and so delicate and most of all so honest. There is no cheating in nature as there is no human society without deceiving.

Dawn itself, the rising of the sun, the dripping of mild rain on thirsty leaves, flowers simply busy blooming, the daily routine of all creatures living in the garden, it all grows into tremendous proportions.

Together all these experiences serve so many moments of happiness, that they build and achieve solid satisfaction for you and ultimate peace and serenity. The same degree of fulfillment can be reached through art, by either creating or simply enjoying it. But then again, isn't it true that artists are very close to nature, seeking refuge there from the oppressive and often suffocating human world? And so once again the natural circle of peace and delight is complete.

Speaking about death, there is a practical question which strikes me. When you die and you are "disposed of", you cease to take up "space". What replaces you? Is it good air, bad air, is it gas? When you were born, you "pushed aside" something, well now it comes back, filling the gap and restoring itself, in a certain way of course. So the ultimate disappearing is an act of creation or at least restoration. What better way to take leave for good!

The Catholic Church is in a crisis once again. Women can never be allowed to be ordained as priests. Where in the Bible does this nonsense originate? Could it possibly be where the Apostles abandoned their wives and children to follow the Master together with their good old buddies? That is when they learned about the high-principled moral of charity, duty and responsibility, which they on their turn were privileged to go and preach the crowd!

Why do so many people consider themselves a genius? They feel like owing it to the less fortunate minds to teach the real truth, knowledge and science. Of course it is so beneficial for the genius himself to know it all beforehand or to have been in the comfortable position of acquiring the whole knowledge easily. Being a genius, then again, offers you an unequalled status which undoubtedly provides you with an attitude of dominating, for the real arrogant even controlling. I from that point of view can consider myself really lucky; I have always been surrounded by geniuses, from the day I was born. Can you imagine the convenience? You never have to reflect and decide what to do. There is always a genius to be found willing to inform you that what you might start to think is wrong and you'd better follow his instructions. So life is made ever so simple and smooth for you, until of course you begin writing this book, shaking off all geniuses at once.

Can you imagine any one defending the abstract theory that everybody is an adventurer, a fortune hunter, deciding and acting out of self-interest. How on earth, in his right and honest mind, can one consider applying this theoretical nonsense to motherhood? Even if mothers take rational decisions anticipating the consequences, they can be left badly bruised and scarred emotionally, completely devastated. From the very moment you become one, being a mother prevails over being the person you are since you were born. In a mother's life her own personal needs and wants are virtually always ignored or overruled by herself for the family's sake. There is no guarantee of happiness though, no guarantee at all, but mothers will always be mothers!

I was touched by a fragment of a dramatic documentary I saw on German television. Big brown bears were shown on their favourite food supply spot. They were all male bears wading the upstream current on the slightly rocky waterfall where salmons fight to jump and conquer the water force in order to swim against the odds and the stream itself. If they make it, they are so exhausted that the only thing they are still capable to do is what they actually came for, to reproduce themselves and then die. Most of the salmons though are easily plucked out of the water by the male bears. These demanding and spoiled creatures only devour the salmons' brain, cheeks and eyes in a proper degustation and then they throw the salmon back in the water. The corpses steer themselves downstream into the claws of lesser gods, wounded or sick male bears that thankfully eat the easy prey to recover as soon as possible. In the meantime the starved mother of two baby-bears is desperately trying to look after the family by both protecting them and searching for food. After, as well as before the mating, she never received any visit or support from the father: they just meet once, he forces himself upon her and then walks away for good into a better life. The mother is not allowed to fish where the catching is easy. She must try her luck more upstream where the surviving salmons from the massacre on the waterfall are scarce. The two cubs are shivering with hunger, fear and weakness. The mother is in agony deciding whether to stay with them and cuddle them or go a little further away to search for food. She decides on the latter only to find one of the cubs been swept away by the water. She desperately swims in search of the little one, spotting his corpse floating in the water. When she carries him out of the water she starts licking him finding out he has been partially devoured by a male bear, maybe even by his own father. The pain and the grief expressed on her face could not be deceptively surpassed by human sorrow. She licks and hugs the mutilated body. Then in a split second a complete change in attitude comes over her and almost perished with hunger she herself attacks the small body and starts eating. Then she stops and takes away the remaining part to the other cub where they both feed themselves on the little victim that never got any chance in life. What a sad story and this cruel world unfortunately is filled with these.

There is a heatwave going on, which is rather unusual in Belgium. The small creatures in the garden as well as bushes and shrubs are starting to suffer. The rhododendrons droop their leaves so they don't catch too much sunlight and warmth; it is a matter of self defense against the aggression of its own kind: it is nature versus nature. As I regrettably live to learn, family can be your worst enemy.

This is summer, the highlight of the year. People are constantly showing off their solarium collected tan in their convertibles. It is amazing how they find any pleasure in demonstrating their summery appearance to people they don't know and that they cross too fast to be noticed by let alone to impress. Mass status is a curious thing, not at all worthwhile. People do their best to try and belong. They worm themselves into an established category, a class, a section in which they feel comfortably accepted and protected by society. When belonging, they every so often pop out to try and surprise their neighbour sections with their materialistic achievements like the right new car or a dramatic plaster sculpture in the lit front garden or their degree of suntan. These are some common status symbols; intellectual achievements, unfortunately, are seldom pursued in their own right, they are only if they can provide material advantages.

The challenge to continuously try and stretch your mind's performance, to further develop your brain's potential seems attractive to so few people within this huge status seeking category, if any at all. They are 'rari nantes' that take pleasure in pure cerebral activity. If you link this intellectual ability and creativity to an artistic insight, you set foot on the breeding ground of mental perfection as far as it is attainable for this mankind and its limitations. Perfection as we comprehend its concept today may be a negligible triviality to future further developed generations.

I find myself as retreating in life's norms and opportunities. Not that I am giving in to a weakening of principles and values, on the contrary I am compiling their use and strength into fewer basic rules. It is like an upside down pyramid. The range and, at the same time, the diversity of insights and regulations on which society is built get compressed into the real musts without any frills, the pillars. These are the bare ethics, esthetics and knowledge, the frame of community.

If I am writing down these wandering thoughts, it is not only to hopefully see them published one day but far more to find a way to reach people that may have been thinking in the same direction. So often I got disillusioned by the poor thinking habit of so many people featuring in my life. By having these thoughts in the open one day, I fervently hope to connect to kindred spirits, even if I never discover who and where they are.

These days it so happens that the Shoemaker Levy 9 comet is crashing down on Jupiter with all of its twenty-one parts. All these striking blows and aftermath of explosions make me look upon the planet as some sort of slain giant with its crushed pride and mutilated force. Of course it will recuperate if only to prove the invincibility of cosmos, which will never allow itself to be destroyed, on the whole or in its fragments, by a violently attacking force, even a minute one, from within. After Jupiter has settled in its new imposed conditions, it even may switch around into a creative spell, surprising us, spectators in awe on earth. With all this and a lot more happening every day, how can people justify to think that they as an individual or even mankind on the whole for that matter, could ever be the centre, the focus, the purpose of universe?

How conceited and presumptuously stupid can you get?

In this light how can one ever defend the right of one person controlling and regulating other people's lives. Isn't this the upmost basic rule that everyone has the right to his own life? It is so sad to experience how some individuals surrounding you claw into your life like a predator. They try and dominate to make up for their own lost opportunities, for their own failure.

Would it be too far-fetched to discover a cosmos in everything that surrounds us? It may well be that every tiny or huge object, living or not, obeys the same cosmos rules. Unfortunately our brain is not yet enough developed to understand, let alone, to apply them. So we could very well be living in a world that on a macro as well as on a micro scale is ruled and regulated by the same basic systems as we speculate universe to be. If that is the case what is bound to happen the minute the human brain dissects these rules? How will human beings fit in to the disclosed cosmos or even better, how will the revealed cosmos respond to human insight? Could human beings eventually manipulate the universe? Or is cosmos coated with self-protection, namely its inscrutable ground rules applicable, in the above theory, on both macro and micro scale? The consequence would be that our brains' function and therefore our minds too are subdued to the same yet unestablished basic rules. So tool and target are as yet restricted in the same manner. How in that case can the tool ever produce the objective unless by a stroke of good luck?

Which harm or misfortune is worse? The self-inflicted one or the one caused by somebody else? What cuts the deepest wounds, self-reproach possibly leading towards self-scorn or having been victimized leading to pent-up rage? The answer of course depends on your personal attitude. For me it is obvious though and will even become more patent if you turn the issue around into a positively founded phrasing: what affects you more, the bunch of flowers you've been offered or the one you bought yourself? It is the extra level of involvement that makes the difference.

When you listen to music, why is it that some combinations of different sounds, simultaneous or not, chords or successive note groups unlock different emotion? There is sad and cheerful music, but why? Sometimes flats reflect melancholy or gloom and sometimes they show deep warmth. Sharps too can reveal either joy or fulfillment and on other occasions they express over-excitement towards screaming madness. What triggers certain emotions? Could it be that the sheer sound strikes the then most vulnerable nerve in our cerebral system? That particular nerve would have become most vulnerable as a sparked off reaction to a whole context of happenings, thoughts and emotions. The reaction can differ, the nerve can differ and so the evoked emotion can differ according to the circumstances.

Since I have been rather dizzy for some time and the real cause has not been detected yet, I try to find a way around this condition. If you would, for instance, take a metaphysical approach, there is this perception of a rotating body in a stand-still world. Is the world real, because of its steadiness? Or is the body real, because of its movement? In other words, is proof of existential essence to be found in immobility or in motion? What is crucial, the being or the evolving, the remaining-the-same or the never-to-be-the-same-again? It is almost like the background on the theatre scene which serves unchanged for various plays, the mountain that endures generations of plantations, the sea that bears centuries of sailing. Is stability the final phase after a journey of evolution or does it, on the contrary, provide the seeding ground for inevitable growth? Or are both needed like day and night, like women and men, like adorning with a mitre?

At this very moment the sky is layered in three marvellous colors, rarely observed together: light grey, violet and apricot: a mighty picturesque combination and, if noticed, even perfectly capable of mollifying mankind.

I have reached the conclusive stage in my perception and reflection of life. Is it because the end is near or is it due to not particularly favourable living conditions but my view on life is rather grim and grisly. And then again not. Life is a void. We get thrown into it by birth and we have to learn to crawl and swim through it in order to survive. Nature and civilisation are acting like features or obstacles capable of either embellishing or reducing the quality of our lives. Some of us create their own water ballet, others thrash about in the water constantly trying to prevent drowning. Again similarity to the cosmos is abundantly clear: voids, black holes, where is the difference? Micro and macro levels of existence are functioning in a comparable way.

What seems to catch my attention is the fact that virtually all of my thinking and possibly any way of thinking, can be reduced to the concept of crossroads. The mere thinking is always carrying a dual aspect to either its train of thought or to its conclusions. The crossroads are not necessarily per se "crossing", they can also be parallel routes or opposite directions for that matter, but the sheer ambiguity is of its essence. Basically it seems to come down to either this or that, like there are two sexes, like there is day and night, fertile and sterile, organic and inorganic, right and left, life and death. Underlining this supposition are the two halves of the brain, two eyes, two ears, two nostrils, two arms and legs, but only one mouth. So, while speaking, we keep the built-in distance in the duality, we maintain the course of the ambiguity while expressing crossing, opposite or parallel thoughts.

Yesterday I experienced an interesting perception. Due to

certain health problems, I am forced to take some medicine. Currently the round and coated tablets have nice and bright pastel colours: there is yellow and sky blue. The vitamins which are supposed to deliver some extra strength and resistance, have a soft apricot hue and present themselves as an oval tablet. Playing with shapes and colours, I found out that perceiving yellow, apricot, blue provided a more satisfying and harmonious sensation than the opposite order of blue, apricot and yellow. My younger daughter attributed this experienced sensation to the western way of reading from left to right. This means an upgrading - which in itself is a positive direction - of the colours from gentle and soft to more explicit. This made me think that varieties of good taste, in a certain way, are linked to cultural inheritance as there is, among other aspects, the basic intellectual ability to read. Inherent might be some substantial differences between western and oriental art.

It is spring again and so there are two of any kind to be found in the garden. Earlier today there was this couple of ducks waddling about from the small pond over the lawn, eventually disappearing underneath some bushes into the wood. If there would have been any clouds at all, they probably would have drifted over in twos. There was still only one sun though. I cannot help developing a sort of déjà-vu feeling together of course with a sense of joy and revival. The bright time is still the right time of the year!

This is the high time of the year too. Two daughters bringing home the most exquisite academic degrees possible. The older daughter graduated from college in the US "magna cum laude", senior year even "summa cum laude" and the younger one finished her first year with distinction ranking at the top 10 of 593 students at Law Leuven University. Leaving college behind her, the older one will now attend Columbia Law School. How proud can a parent get?

This was supposed to be a terrible night though. Not being able to attend a family occasion, I had to spend the night all by myself, with a lot of pain due to a Sudeck atrophy and sciatica and a thunderstorm passing. Completely overwhelmed by those awful circumstances which could be described as of the worst kind, I started to play the piano. Then I decided to listen to the old favourites van Beethoven and

Rachmaninov while writing this down. The night is still young but, so far so good. I survive.

A few months later, the Sudeck is still around, the thunderstorm has gone, as you might have guessed.

Very frustrating is the thought that it just might be possible that everything there is to know is "floating" around us. We simply have to instruct our brain to reach out and grab the knowledge or the information to achieve it. Our brain, however, is not yet developed or trained enough to grasp the necessary signals. It is like a well-equipped lab where the apparatus is not switched on. Some people sometimes have the ability to "dive" into this "stream" of "laws and regulations", of "truth and order". They are either genius or clairvoyant. Most of us though build their knowledge through hard work, based on a certain degree of sheer study-zeal. Future generations will progress in building brain capacity and -aptitude to pick the omnipresent and universal knowledge as needed. But, if people are able to possess knowledge in a fingers' snap, how on earth (?!) will they fill up all the spare time?

What is it that people like to read most and, more importantly, invites them to think? Is it a fully spun and spread philosophical theory on a logical scale or is it a whole range, a spectrum of thoughts based on a daily experience of events and subsequent conclusions and emotions? Only in the latter case of course can this book ever turn out to be satisfactory.

I tried a literary fugue out of the surrounding jungle.

Leap in time! Today, 10 July 2020, the world has become an even bigger jungle as global problems add up each day: politics, covid-19, climate change, BLM...

How can we not be concerned, terrified about our children's and grandchildren's future? Let us fervently hope that they can find ways to solve the problems, cure the drawbacks and be happy again!

Lightning Source UK Ltd.
Milton Keynes UK
UKHW010810111220
374897UK00002B/400